Jesus, This Is Your Life

Stories & Pictures by Kids

Edited by Jeff Kunkel

"Unless you become like a little child,
you will never enter the realm of God."
—Jesus of Nazareth

"This is Jesus standing in front of the Jordan River."
Joseph Rueter, age 12

To Sean and Patrick Johnson,
great artists, good friends, able assistants

"Jesus is on a boat at sea in a terrible storm, but he is asleep with a smile on his face because he trusts God to take care of him. His trust in God is also what makes the halo around his head."
—Carolyn Lees, age 10

JESUS, THIS IS YOUR LIFE
Stories and Pictures by Kids

Copyright © 2001 Jeff Kunkel.

Scripture passages are from the New Revised Standard Version of the Bible, copyright © 1946, 1952, 1971, 1989 by the Division of Christian Education of the National Council of the Churches of Christ in the USA. Used by permission.

Cover design by Laurie Ingram Duran, Inc.; Book design by Michelle L. Norstad

ISBN 0-8066-4165-7

The paper used in this publication meets the minimum requirements of American National Standard for Information Sciences—Permanence of Paper for Printed Library Materials, ANSI Z329.48-1984. ∞™

Manufactured in Singapore   AF 9-4165

05   04   03   02   01   1   2   3   4   5   6   7   8   9   10

Contents

Introduction

Long ago and far away in a place called Israel, a baby boy was born and given the name Jesus. Jesus learned to speak Aramaic, the language used by his parents and neighbors in his boyhood village, Nazareth. He also learned to speak and read Hebrew in the synagogue, where his family worshiped the Lord God of Israel.

Jesus grew up and became such a remarkable man that people followed him everywhere he went. Because of his words and deeds, Jesus' followers believed that he was the Messiah whom God had promised. These followers began to tell stories about what Jesus said and did, and about what happened to him. After Jesus died, his followers wrote down these stories so that other people could learn about him. These stories were collected in the Bible. The Bible is the best-selling book of all time and has been translated into most of the languages used on earth.

As a child, I first learned the Bible stories about the life of Jesus. As a grown-up, I have studied these stories. In my work as an author, artist, and minister, I have shared these stories with children from many different churches, races, and backgrounds. Such children are the artists and writers of this book. They were between the ages of five and twelve at the time.

In my workshops, I chose a Bible story that told about an important event in Jesus' life and gave the children something to see, smell, hear, taste, or touch. A child can see Zacchaeus up in that sycamore tree. A child can

"Jesus, with pink perfume dripping from his head."
—Ceri Freedman, age 10

hear the angry crowd shout, "Crucify him!" A child can smell Simon Peter's dirty feet just before Jesus washes them. I read each story aloud and asked a child to read it aloud a second time.

Next, I invited the children to write the story in their own words and then draw or paint the story as they imagined it. This allowed each child to respond to the story in many ways–through word, image, shape, color, memory, and feeling. At the end of each session, I displayed the stories and pictures at an art opening, with conversation, refreshments, parents, and friends.

The children's stories and artwork inspired me to share their work with a larger audience, so I put together an exhibition of artwork, "Jesus, This Is Your Life." This exhibition traveled to many churches and hospitals and entertained thousands of people.

Now the children's work will reach even more people. This book includes information about the writers and artists and the biblical reference for each story so that you can also read the accounts in a Bible.

The children's stories and pictures are fresh, brave, and true–and sure to make you laugh, frown, wonder, and trust. Enjoy!

Jeff Kunkel

Jeff Kunkel

"And a little child shall lead them."
—Isaiah 11:6

Jesus loves me! This I know,
as he loved so long ago,
taking children on his knee,
saying, "Let them come to me."
—verse 2 of traditional song, "Jesus Loves Me"

Jesus Is Born

Luke 2:1-20
written by Joseph Rueter, age 12

Joseph and Mary rode across the desert on a little donkey. By the time they got to Bethlehem, it was dark and cold. There was only one hotel in Bethlehem, which they called an inn. Joseph knocked on the door and a man opened it and said, "What do you want?"

Joseph said, "We want a room."

The man said, "Sorry. All my rooms are full tonight."

Joseph said, "But Mary, my wife, is about to have a baby!"

The man said, "There's a stable down the street where the animals sleep. It smells bad, but it's warm and dry. You can stay there."

Joseph and Mary and their donkey went to the stable, and Mary had her baby there. She wrapped the baby in a blanket to keep him warm and put him in a manger on top of some soft hay.

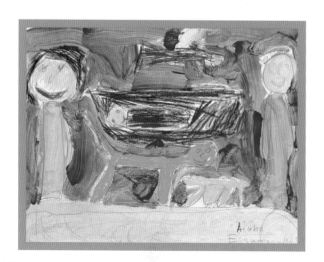

"Jesus' baby picture with his mom and dad, an angel, and his animal friends all around him."
—Aisha Essuman-Mensah, age 10

Near Bethlehem in a field, shepherds guarded their sheep from wolves and thieves. An angel appeared to the shepherds, and they were scared. But the angel said, "Don't be afraid—your king was born in Bethlehem. His name is Jesus. You will find him lying in a manger. Go see him!"

8

"The star of Bethlehem shining down
on the stable where Jesus was just born."
—Howard Marcus, age 11

Where Is That Boy?

Luke 2:41-52
written by Riley Morgan, age 10

When Jesus was 12 years old, he went to Jerusalem with his mom and dad. The only way to get there was to walk, so they walked for a couple of days across the desert. Jerusalem was crowded with people when they got there because of a holy party called Passover. His mother said to Jesus, "Don't go wandering off or you'll get lost!"

But Jesus wanted to see the temple, so he wandered off into the crowd.

His parents looked all over for Jesus but could not find him. His dad said, "We've looked everywhere in Jerusalem!"

His mom said, "No. We haven't looked in the temple."

So his parents ran to the temple and found Jesus sitting with the old men and asking questions about God. His mom was happy to find Jesus, but she was also mad. She said, "Jesus, I told you not to wander off! We thought something bad happened to you!"

The three of them left the city and didn't say much all the way home.

"The Temple of Jerusalem."
—Becky Johnson, age 10

"Jesus' mom and dad are coming back to the city to look for Jesus.
They will find him in the yellow temple."
—Riley Morgan, age 10

Jesus' Baptism

Mark 1:1-11
written by Alexandra Fisher, age 8

Jesus was coming, and John was excited. "Jesus is coming!" John was yelling. "Jesus is much greater than I, yet I get to baptize him."

That night, John went to pray.

The next day, Jesus went down to the Jordan River with John. John put Jesus in the water and baptized him.

God spoke to Jesus from heaven and said, "I love you, Son."

A dove flew down with a message for John. It read: "Thanks for baptizing me. Your friend, Jesus."

The End

"Jesus is underwater and dressed in black. The yellow is God showing Jesus the way to heaven. All the birds flew off when God came down."
—Jesus Rios, age 10

"John baptizes Jesus at night, under the stars.
The cross on the mountain waits for Jesus."
—Tony Falkowski, age 10

Satan and Jesus: A Skit

Luke 4:1-13
written by Gene Cushing, age 12

Jesus, wearing white, enters stage right, followed by Satan, dressed in black.

Satan: "Are you hungry?"

Jesus: "Yes."

Satan: "If you follow me, you can go into any store and get all the food you want—for free."

Jesus: "You can't live on chips alone."

Narrator: Satan then took Jesus to the top of the Empire State Building.

Satan: "If you are the Son of God, jump off this building and the angels will save you."

Jesus: "You should not test the Lord."

Satan, getting mad: "Look down. See all that? My gang is in charge of it all. If you join me, I'll let you run all of it. Deal?"

Jesus: "No way. And if you don't leave me alone, I'll call God."

Satan: "You're impossible!"

"The devil is standing in the fiery pits of hell. He has an evil smile and green eyes, because green stands for envy."
—Carolyn Lees, age 10

"Jesus is in the desert, trying to be with God.
The devil comes up to him on a T-Rex, holding up his pitchfork
and a Hershey's chocolate bar to get Jesus' attention."
—Gene Cushing, age 12

Following Jesus

Luke 5:1-11
written by Skye Wilson, age 11

Jesus was preaching God's word, and people were crowding up to him. He saw two boats on the beach and nearby fishermen were washing their nets. Jesus went down to the beach and got into one of the boats, which belonged to two men, Simon and Peter. He told them to push the boat out into the water. From there, he preached to the crowd on land. When he was finished, Jesus told Simon and Peter to row the boat out to deeper water. Once they were there he told them to let down the nets. "My Master," one of them said, "We worked very hard all of last night and didn't catch any fish, but since you say so, we will." They let down the nets and when they pulled them in they were full of fish. In fact, the fish filled both boats, theirs and their friend's. Both men bowed down on their knees and said, "Lord, please go away. We are sinful men and don't deserve to be with you."

But Jesus said, "You will no longer catch fish. You will catch men and women." They rowed back to shore and, leaving everything, followed Jesus.

The End

"This is Jesus' boat in the ocean, far from land. He's flying the Tongan flag."
—John Katoa, age 11

16

"Simon Peter in his boat, catching fish."
—Tina Katoa, age 10

Some Children Come Close to Jesus

Mark 10:13-16
written by Rebecca Corbett, age 11
and
christine villamarin, age 11

Some children tried to get close to Jesus, but his disciples scolded the children and said, "Go away!"

Jesus said, "No! Let the children come close to me." He blessed the children and patted each one on the shoulder.

After the children left, he said to the disciples, "Those children trusted me. Do you?"

"Jesus is blessing the children by putting his hands on their heads."
—Stephanie Jala, age 10

18

"Mothers are bringing their kids to Jesus."
—Jessica Horton, age 11

The Man Who Could Not Walk

Mark 2:1-12
written by Zachary Garmen, age 6

There once was a man who could not walk. Lucky for him, he had some good friends. His friends heard that Jesus was at a nearby house, so they carried the man who could not walk to that house. It was crowded like crazy. They got the man up on the roof and cut a hole in it. Then they put the man on his mat and lowered him through the hole. Jesus said to the man, "Get up and walk!"

The man got up and walked away.

The people in the house said, "Wow!"

"Jesus about to heal the
man who could not walk."
—Scott O'Neil, age 10

"Inside and outside the house with the hole in the roof."
—Stephanie Sheppard, age 11

The Raging Storm

Matthew 8:23-27
written by Alexandra Fisher, age 8

Jesus and his followers were in a boat. All of a sudden a storm struck. The waves got big and fat and rocked the boat, but Jesus was asleep and did not wake up. His followers went to him and said, "Jesus! Wake up! There is a big storm, and we are all going to die!"

Jesus awoke and said, "You don't have much faith. We will live!"

Jesus got up on deck and held his arms up high and told the storm to stop, and it did. His followers were very surprised and said, "He is so powerful even the wind and waves obey him!"

The End

"The boat in the storm, with Jesus down below, asleep on a mat."
—Sione Kahausa, age 11

"Jesus is awake now, standing in the bow of the boat,
facing the storm with his cowardly disciples behind him."
—Billy Estell, age 11

Jesus on Top of a Mountain

Mark 9:2-8
written by Ahna Veurink, age 10

Jesus took his three best friends, Simon Peter, James, and John, and led them up a high mountain in the middle of the desert. When Jesus got to the top, his clothes began to sparkle and glow with light. Then Jesus began to talk with the spirits. His three friends got scared and asked Jesus, "Who are you talking to?"

Jesus said, "To Moses and Elijah."

His friends didn't know what to do, so they got busy and put up three tents—one for Jesus, one for Moses, and one for Elijah. A cloud in the sky drifted by the mountain, and God spoke from the cloud, "This is my Son. Listen to what he tells you!"

"While on the mountain, Jesus' disciples put up three tents for Jesus, Moses, and Elijah."
—Scott O'Neil, age 10

"Jesus is on top of the mountain and
listening to the voice of God in the cloud."
—Ahna Veurink, age 10

Two Sisters

Luke 10:38-41
written by Katie Reutter, age 7

Once upon a time there were two sisters. Their names were Mary and Martha. One day Mary was praying with Jesus, and Martha was working hard. Martha got mad and said, "Jesus, ask my sister to help me with the work or I'll never get it all done!"

Jesus said, "No. Mary is doing the right thing. Leave her alone."

"That's Martha, Mary, and Jesus."
—Tyler Garmen, age 5

"Mary is praying, and Martha is doing all the chores.
Jesus is saying, "Mary is doing the right thing."
—Katie Reutter, age 7

Where's My Sheep?

Luke 15:1-7
written by Skye Wilson, age 11

The followers of Jesus argued about which one of them was the best, so Jesus told them this story: "There was a shepherd who had 100 sheep. One day he counted his sheep as usual but only counted 99. He thought to himself, "What does one sheep matter since I still have 99?" But in his heart he knew he was wrong and packed himself a lunch. He left his 99 sheep alone and went looking for the lost sheep. He looked everywhere but didn't find his sheep until dusk. He was so happy that he put the sheep on his shoulders and carried it all the way home. He then told everybody in town and went home to care for his 100 sheep."

The End

"This scale shows that 1 sheep
can equal 99 sheep."
—Michael O'Malley, age 11

"The shepherd has left his flock and is looking for his lost sheep."
—Skye Wilson, age 11

A Bad Man Becomes a Good Man

Luke 19:1-10
written by Alysandre Saavedra, age 8

Zacchaeus was a short man who wanted to see what Jesus looked like, but many tall people crowded around Jesus. So, Zacchaeus climbed a tree in order to see Jesus. Jesus came by, looked up at Zacchaeus in the tree, and said, "Zacchaeus, you come down here! I've got to stay in your house today!"

The people did not like this because they knew that Zacchaeus was a bad man.

Zacchaeus climbed down the tree, took Jesus to his house, and said, "I will give half of what I own to the poor, and if I have cheated anyone, I will give them back four times as much!"

Jesus went out and said to the people, "Zacchaeus was a bad man, but he has changed, and now he is a good man, but still short."

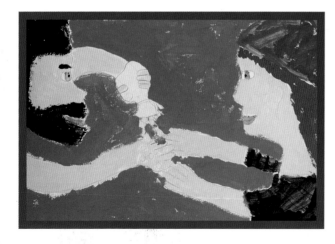

"Zacchaeus is giving his money away to this poor woman."
—Linnea Nasman, age 10

30

"Little man Zacchaeus high in a tree,
trying to get a glimpse of Jesus."
—Paige Harkness, age 9

Jesus Gets Mad

Luke 19:45-48
written by Christine Ledford, age 11

Jesus went into the temple and found a guy selling valuables like wine, jugs of water, and bottles of perfume. Jesus got mad at the guy and said to him, "The temple is supposed to be for praying, not making money!"

Each day after that, Jesus went to the temple and taught the people about God, and the people ate up every word.

"The guy on the left is the Temple Guy, who is selling valuables in the temple. Jesus is the guy on the right with the beard."
—Christine Ledford, age 11

"Jesus is turning over the tables in the temple,
and the caged birds are flying free."
—Robin Miller, age 10

The Pool That Healed

John 5:1-4
written by Sarah Anaya, age 9

A long time ago, there was a healing pool called Bethzatha. People would go there to have their sickness go away. All sorts of people went to that healing pool— blind people, paralyzed people, and a man who had been sick for 38 years. Every time this man would try to get into the pool, someone would step in front of him. Finally, Jesus saw him lying there on his mat and asked him, "Do you want your sickness to be healed?"

The man said, "Yes, please."

Jesus said, "Grab your mat, stand up, and walk!"

"I painted all kinds and colors of mats. They are all empty because no one is sick any more—Jesus healed them all."
—Chris Sukup, age 10

"I show the guys in the healing pool on mats and inner tubes.
Others are waiting to get into the pool when they can fit."
—Jessica Williams, age 9

The Poor Widow

Mark 12:38-44
written by Katie Reutter, age 7

Jesus sat down by the temple and watched the people put their money into the temple money pot. Rich people put in bags of gold coins, but then a poor widow came by and put in two little coins. Jesus said, "She has given her last two coins to the temple money pot, which is more than the rich people gave." This made Jesus happy.

"A rich man dropping his gold coins into the temple treasury."
—Ceri Freedman, age 10

"Jesus watching a widow put her two coins in the temple bank.
They are both happy."
—Lesley Hollingsworth, age 10

Dirty Feet

John 13:1-9
written by Andrea Carter, age 9

Jesus filled a big bowl with water and asked his followers to gather around the bowl. Jesus began to wash their dirty feet, but Simon Peter would not let Jesus wash his feet. He said to Jesus, "You shouldn't wash my feet. I should wash your feet!"

But Jesus said, "If I wash away the dirt and stink from your feet, your sins will also be washed away."

Simon Peter said, "Then wash my feet. And wash my arms and my legs and my head, too!"

"The bucket of water that Jesus used to wash his disciples' feet."
—Tammy Hinds, age 10

"These feet are bloody, dirty, and stinky,
but Jesus can wash all of that away."
—Andrea Carter, age 9

His Last Supper

Luke 22:14-23
written by Aisha Ivery, age 10

Jesus and his disciples got together for supper, as usual. They all sat around a big table, ready to eat. Jesus knew that he was going to die soon, so he stood, broke a loaf of bread in two, and said, "This is *my* body, given for you." Jesus passed the bread around, then lifted a cup filled with wine and said, "This is *my* blood, shed for you." He passed the cup around and sat down. That was his last supper on earth.

"Drink and eat this bread in memory of me."
—Tyler Garmen, age 4

"My picture shows families at the supper table—daddies and mommies and girls and boys. Jesus is holding up the bread and wine to bless it."
—Imani Ivery, age 6

Thrown in Jail

Matthew 26:47-56
written by Aisha Essuman-Mensah, age 10

Jesus had lots of friends, but he had some enemies, too. His enemies wanted to get rid of him, because they were jealous of how many people liked Jesus. One enemy by the name of Judas told lies about Jesus to the police and led them right to Jesus.

A policeman grabbed Jesus and said, "We have to arrest you!"

One of Jesus' friends said, "No way!" He pulled out his sword and cut off the policeman's ear!

Jesus said, "Put your sword away and don't hurt anyone else. If I need help, I will ask God to send me an army of angels."

All of Jesus' friends left him and ran away, and the police arrested Jesus and threw him in jail.

"One of the guys with Jesus cut off the ear of one of the guys who came to take Jesus away."
—Chris Goodness, age 8

"Jesus got arrested and put in this jail."
—Aisha Essuman-Mensah, age 10

Jesus Dies on the Cross

Luke 23:32-49
written by Amira Essuman-Mensah, age 7

On a beautiful day, Jesus was carried away by soldiers to a place called The Skull. He was forced to carry a big wooden cross, and he was laughed at and made fun of. The soldiers hung Jesus on his cross in the hot sun, and did the same with two other men. The sun disappeared from the sky and it got dark as night for three long hours, from noon until three o'clock. Jesus looked up and shouted, "God, take my spirit to heaven!" Then he died.

The End

"When Jesus got put on the cross, the sun turned black."
—Ceri Freedman, age 10

"It got dark as midnight when Jesus died on the cross. The hands of God are coming down from above to take back his spirit."
—Darcy Shiber-Knowles, age 11

Jesus Rises from the Dead

Matthew 28:1-8
written by Alysandre Saavedra, age 8

After Jesus was crucified, his body was put in a grave. One Sunday morning, two women both named Mary came to see Jesus and pray for him. Suddenly, the ground shook under their feet and an angel of the Lord came down out of the white clouds. His clothes were even whiter than the clouds and he looked like lightning and thunder. The men guarding the grave got so scared they fell over, ready to die, but the angel didn't let them die.

The angel said to the women, "Fear me not! I know you are looking for Jesus. He is not here. He has gone ahead of you to Galilee. Go tell his followers to meet him there."

The two Marys ran away from the grave in order to tell the others about what they had seen and heard. They were afraid but also filled with hope.

"This picture shows the empty tomb made of white stone. An angel has rolled away the giant stone door and is standing inside the tomb. One of his wings is damaged from a battle with the devil. The area around the tomb is a green garden with berry patches, a pond, and trees casting shadows."
—Neil Ose, age 8

"An angel is rolling away the stone to show that Jesus is no longer in the tomb, that he rose from the dead and is okay. Jesus' bed is still in the tomb, but it is empty. The yellow cross in the background where Jesus hung is also empty."
—Madison McCormick, age 8

Writers and Artists

"Jesus alone on the cross, with yellow stars."
—Andrea Leeds, age 10